TWO OF A KIND

First presented by Bill Kenwright in association with the ThorndikeTheatre, Leatherhead and the Theatre Royal, Windsor, on 25th July 1995 at the Theatre Royal, Windsor, with the following cast:

"Wally" Wallis	Eric Sykes
George Fairbrother	Michael Denison
May	Dulcie Gray
Matron	Carmen Silvera

Directed by Ian Kellgren
Designed by Geoffrey Scott
Lighting designed by Matt Drury
Associate Producer Rod Coton

An earlier version of the play titled **THE DIVIDER** was presented by the Casson Company at the Casson Room, Thorndike Theatre on 16th May 1985 with the following cast:

George	Alan White
Matron	Muriel Barker
May	Freda Jackson
Wally	Peter Baylis

Directed by Alan Rothwell
Designed by Stuart Stanley

Two of a Kind

A comedy

Hugh Janes

Samuel French — London
New York - Toronto - Hollywood

Please see page iv for further copyright information

Printed in Great Britain by Redwood Books Limited, Trowbridge, Wiltshire

CHARACTERS

"Wally" Wallis
Major George Fairbrother
Matron
May

The action of the play takes place in the lobby, the Matron's office, and a shared room in the Grove Lodge Retirement Home. Scenes in the Chapel of Rest and Garden are set in the lobby area

Time — the present. Spring

ACT I — Saturday and Sunday

ACT II — Monday and Tuesday

This play is dedicated to
Bill and Rod,
without whom ...

ACT I

Grove Lodge Retirement Home. Saturday

The home has been converted from a large old house with some original features still intact. To one side is a plain room slightly too small for two residents: this is Wally's room. It has easy chairs, set as if used by friends, divan beds, bedside cabinets and lamps, a double wardrobe (with a plate on top of it), chest of drawers, waste-basket and wash-basin. A curtained window overlooks the garden. A shelf beside Wally's bed has on it three worn paperbacks, Jane's Fighting Ships, *a large seashell and an old photo of friends on a ship. Under Wally's bed is an old trunk and a kitbag. The shelf by the other bed has on it a garish beer mug and a soccer scarf. A ship's bell is mounted beside the shelf*

A half-door leads from the bedroom into a lobby with a hall table, fire hydrant and noticeboard. Two corridors lead off the lobby: one past the door to Matron's office, the other to an unseen dining area. There is also a fire exit door. A large, smart suitcase stands on the lobby floor

US *of the lobby is Matron's fresh, smart office with a palm, filing cabinet and desk with chairs either side. The window has attractive curtains. An old attaché case stands on top of the filing cabinet. Matron's office may be raised and linked with stairs up from the lobby to the corridor*

When the CURTAIN *rises, the Lights are on in all the areas. Matron, middle-aged and crisply attired, stands in the bedroom, holding a clipboard and examining the room*

In the office, George, a man hidebound by order and convention, is waiting. He has with him a hat and furled umbrella

Matron removes the scarf and mug from the shelf and walks to her office. She hangs the scarf over the old attaché case and puts the mug beside it. She picks up a clean towel

Matron If you follow me, Colonel Fairbrother, I'll show you to your room.
George Thank you, Matron. Actually it's Major.
Matron (*checking her clipboard*) Major. Oh. This way.

George picks up his hat and umbrella and follows. In the corridor he picks up his large, smart suitcase. Matron stops in the lobby and indicates an unseen room out front

Matron Now, what do you think of this?

George Oh, most attractive.

Matron This is the standard we set in all our rooms.

George I shall be more than happy in here.

Matron You're not in here; this is Mrs Gleason's. I wanted you to see what yours will look like when it's been modernized. (*They move on*) The room you're in now compensates with a very pleasant view of the garden.

They enter the room; George is disappointed

There. Home sweet home. This room has the morning sun. Mr Wallis, who sleeps there, has been here four years now. An outgoing person, friendly — with most people, so you should get on like houses on fire.

George I was expecting a single.

Matron And you would be in one now if Mr Gomez hadn't brought your ceiling down with his bath water. Our builder estimates only six to eight weeks.

George drops his case with a thud

If Mr Potterton hadn't passed on this morning you wouldn't even have this. We try not to be oppressive here at Grove Lodge: "care is the watchword". No reflection on yourself but some people of advancing years sit alone and get morbid.

George We can get as morbid as we like in groups, can we?

Matron I like to have everyone mixing. A cocktail party, minus cocktails.

George I see.

Matron We run many activities; bingo, beetle drives and the vicar leads an excellent game of "Oh Hell". The church is a great provider but then we do encourage religion.

George I've rather lapsed I'm afraid. Surfeit of church parades. (*He puts his case, hat and umbrella on his bed and removes his overcoat*)

Matron We'll soon unlapse you. There are two television rooms and a "quiet" lounge at the end, where knitting needles are forbidden. An excellent place to write one's memoirs.

George Do many people write their memoirs?

Matron Oh I've a cupboard stuffed with Chapter Ones.

George I'm on chapter four of a detective novel.

Matron Fiction. We're not used to such ambition.

George "The Case for Justin Lockett". He's a sort of modern day Raffles. Lockett, you see, the key is in his name.

Matron Good; activity will stop you from nodding off during the day. I allow a nap after lunch, if you can't stop yourself. Any more only spoils your sleep. Food, alcohol and smoking in the room are absolutely taboo. Tipsy old people falling down starting fires make a lot of extra work. We haven't time to waste extinguishing scorched pensioners.

George No.

Matron You are allowed out — whenever you have my permission. You will make your own bed and keep the room generally tidy. Sheets and towels are changed every Monday unless they become particularly soiled. Should you become incontinent don't keep it a secret between yourself and the mattress, we are organized in that department.

George I assure you, Matron ...

Matron Everyone does, Major. Everyone does. All seems a bit of a rush I expect? How long have you been on our waiting list?

George Over six months. Since I first saw your advertisement.

Matron So few places arise. We take pride in prolonging life. (*She glances at George's bed*) As a rule.

George Everything sounded right for me here. The right setting. The right type of people.

Matron Oh yes. I can see you're going to fit in. That's what counts.

A pager on her belt bleeps

Oh, my pager. Minor crisis. Do excuse me.

She exits

George sits dejectedly on the corner of his bed and surveys the room

George Oh damn! (*He rises and hangs his coat in the wardrobe, puts his hat on top and hangs the umbrella on the side nearest his bed*)

May enters. She is a well-dressed, determined woman who walks aided by a stick. She passes Matron's office and starts singing "Isn't It a Lovely Day to Be Caught in the Rain"

As May sings, George opens his case and stands listening to the song. Then he places two family photographs, a framed display of medals and a few detective novels on his shelf and hangs a blazer and trousers in the wardrobe

May clicks her tongue three times and wiggles her hips. She checks no-one is about and opens the fire exit door

May (*calling off*) Wally?

Matron crosses the lobby with a vase of flowers

May hides

Matron enters the room

Matron I thought under the circumstances the room could do with brightening up.
George What lovely flowers. Are they from the garden?
Matron No. The crematorium.
George Oh.
Matron Some kind of exchange I suppose. We're like a florists here in winter. Unpacking? That's it, set out your stall. No point shilly-shallying around. Life's abysmally short as it is. A soldier and a literary man; I'll introduce you to our expert on crossword puzzles — and our war widows.
George One or two introductions would be more than sufficient. I'm not particularly gregarious.
Matron We'll sort you out, don't worry. (*She goes out of the room*)
George (*following*) Oh Matron? I wonder, could you ... the ... wash room.
Matron Jolly good. No messing about. Come along.
May (*returning to the fire exit and calling out of the door*) Wally.
Matron May? Whatever are you doing?
May (*surprised*) Nothing, Matron.
Matron You look as if you're loitering.
May I have never loitered in my life.
Matron You'll do your arthritis no favours hanging around draughty doors. (*She shuts the fire door*)
May Don't shut the door. (*Fabricating*) I was just catching my breath. (*She breathes heavily*)
Matron That's why we're here. To help with these little problems. (*She takes May's arm*)
May There is no problem and I don't want to go anywhere.
Matron Come along now, May.
May (*not moving; to George*) Are you him?
George Him?
May Is he? Is he him?
Matron Now, May ...
May I do not like being manhandled; especially by a woman.
Matron Now come along.
May Will you let go? I must be here. It's important.
Matron Be quiet, there's a good girl. You wouldn't want me to call Nurse Wiggins.

May Oh gawd!

She exits immediately

Matron Just along there, Major. Door with the "little man".
George Thank you. (*He pauses, puzzled by May*)
Matron You'll be all right will you? Don't need any help?
George Oh no. (*He heads for the exit*)

Matron exits

There is banging on the fire door

George stops and looks

Wally (*off*) May! Open the blooming door. What's the matter, you silly old coot.

George listens at the door

George Hallo?
Wally May, stop messing about and open this door.

George tentatively opens the door

Wally bustles in. He is a dishevelled seadog in old nautical clothes. One of life's contenders

Where's that silly fool May? Matron could have caught me. Ay ay, new face straight off the ferry. When were you admitted?
George Today.
Wally We need some young blood about the place. House is full of pensioners.
George (*surveying Wally*) Do you live here?
Wally Yes I do.
George (*shutting the door*) I beg your pardon but you can't be too careful these days. I didn't want to admit anyone.
Wally They admitted you. I suppose you're private.
George I'm paying, yes.
Wally You look private. I'm Council. One of the last. Doesn't half stick in Matron's craw.
George There appears to be something oozing under your arm.
Wally (*removing a steak, wrapped in paper, from under his arm*) Ssh! Don't breath a word.

George I wasn't going to.

Wally Contraband, that's what this is. Smuggled. Only they have Customs and Excise men in here dressed up as nurses.

George Do they?

Wally (*unwrapping the steak*) 'Ere, look at that. Isn't that a nice bit of steak? Aberdeen Angus. Well, late Aberdeen Angus. Proper steak that is, not the mad cow they have in here.

George I'm a vegetarian myself.

Wally Last vegetarian we had suffocated on an omelette. (*He taps his gullet*) A pimento blocked his sarcophagus. I tell you, it's lame dogs and Englishmen in here.

George Sounds like I'm in for a stimulating decline.

Wally Potts is the life and soul of this place. Bloke I bunk with. Even Matron likes Potts and she's not a woman to give her affections lightly. I take it you've met Mrs Winstanley (*née* Hitler) SRN?

George She was extremely kind.

Wally Kind? She'd throw a drowning man both ends of the rope.

George I'll try not to slip in the bath then. (*He gives a little laugh*)

Wally It's no laughing matter. Matron is the senior citizens' Captain Bligh. Duck when you hear her keys rattling.

George She doesn't lock you in, does she?

Wally No, she throws them at you. (*He slaps the back of his head*) One volley and Good-night Vienna!

George I take it you don't like authority.

Wally I'm used to it but the day I stop challenging it is the day I pop off. I'm only here because the Old Sailors' Retirement Home was full of retired old sailors.

George Will you excuse me. I have to find the little man.

Wally Know him well.

George And don't worry about your steak, I'm very good at secrets. (*He heads off*)

Wally Keeping them — or telling them?

George The former. I signed the Official Secrets Act you know.

He exits quickly

Wally Don't hurry, old son. You've just joined the queue for the hereafter — and there's not much of a rush to get to the front.

May enters

May Pssst!

Wally I expect you are.

May You got in then.

Wally No, I'm still outside. That's the last time I ask you to do me a favour.

May Wally, I have something important to tell you.

Wally Some weak-bladdered toffee-nose let me in. So I expect all our undercover operations are blown.

May Please listen. It's serious.

Wally (*whistling*) Pipe up, Potts. Shipwrecked sailor coming aboard.

May Don't go in there.

Wally enters the room

Oh, please yourself.

May walks away

Wally looks about the room and returns to the lobby, confused

Wally I'm in the right place. Cell block 17. 'Ere, May, have you seen Potts? There's a suitcase out. Do you think he's going on his holidays?

May How the hell should I know. I'm not Thomas Cook.

May exits

Wally (*entering the room*) More like Captain Cook. Silly old sea buzzard. Where's his things? He's only got enough to fill a paper bag.

Wally discards the steak on to his bed and looks in George's case. It has layers of laundered, good quality shirts, ties, etc. Wally burrows into them, strewing clothes everywhere

George enters

George What in God's name do you think you are doing?

Wally Unravelling a mystery old son. Went out this morning and left my old mucker in his hammock with a touch of bronchials. Come back and the Marie Celeste is deserted. I wondered if these were his things?

George Those are my things. That is my case.

Wally What's it doing here?

George This is my room. I'm unpacking.

George tidies his clothes; Wally puts them back in the case. George takes them out; Wally puts them back

Wally No don't — don't unpack, old son. You're in the wrong room. You are the victim of a bureaucratic balls-up.

George Matron herself put me in here.

Wally Poor woman's going doo-lally. All this mixing with old folk. Me and Potts been in here four years. She can't go chopping and changing just like that now, can she?

George Are you ... Mr Wallis?

Wally No mister in my name, I'm just Wally.

George It might be advisable if you went to see Matron.

Wally What is this? What's going on?

George I would prefer not to say.

Wally There's a plate on top of the wardrobe. Fix my steak to it. And no nibbling while I'm out.

Wally plonks the steak in George's hand and leaves, heading for the door to Matron's office. George puts the steak on the plate

The Lights fade in the room

During the following, George removes his suit jacket and hangs it over the back of an easy chair. He then moves the chair beside his bed, in front of the wardrobe

Matron enters and meets Wally outside her office

Matron, what's happened to ——

Matron Ah there you are, Mr Wallis. I've been looking for you. (*She opens her office door*)

They enter the office

You've been out again without permission.

Wally I've been round the world twenty times, I think I can manage half a day at the shops.

Matron Suppose something happens to you?

Wally Something usually does. (*He shuts the door*)

Matron (*sitting at her desk*) Missing meals ruins the continuity of our diet.

Wally I don't like this Saturday cook.

Matron Mr Pyranjanis was trained at the Savoy.

Wally What as? Hall porter?

Matron Please sit down, Mr Wallis.

Wally I like standing. Takes the weight off my bum.

Matron It is extremely difficult for me to tell you this. Sadly, Mr Potterton passed on this morning.

Wally Potts? Passed on? Don't be daft, woman. Potts wouldn't pass on without telling me where he was going. He'd tell me wouldn't he?

Matron It was very sudden.

Wally Sudden. There was nothing wrong with him. He was in good health. Touch of the bronchials, that's all. Bit of a chill on the chest. Look, I bought him some vapour rub. (*He takes a pot of Vick from his pocket and puts it on his desk*)

Matron Something like this leaves everyone unprepared.

Wally Tell me you've just moved him to another room — temporary like.

Matron I wish it was that simple.

Slowly the news of the death sinks in to Wally

Wally (*picking up the Vick*) He won't be needing this, then.

Matron I'm afraid not.

Wally removes his woolly hat and sits

It was a heart attack. The chest complaint may have been an early symptom. I went in to see him shortly after you'd gone out. It had already happened. The ambulance arrived within minutes but it was no use. Took us all completely by surprise.

Wally Where is he, Matron?

Matron I'm not sure exactly.

Wally That's typical of Potts to go missing at a time like this.

Matron I mean — by now he may be with the undertaker.

Wally Discussing terms?

Matron His relatives made some mention of him being bur ——

Wally Relatives? If you mean Nora the niece, I'm amazed she remembered who you were talking about.

Matron Families have different ways of staying close. Blood is thicker than water.

Wally Gin is thicker than her blood. (*He sees Potts' things*) Are these his things, Matron?

Matron Yes.

Wally That's his mug. (*He picks it up*) He won this at Blackpool fun fair. Took some girl there on a day trip and tried to win her a teddy bear on the rifle range. All he got was this. He was a rotten shot. God knows why they took him in the Royal Artillery. He never drank out of anything else. Used to carry it from pub to pub. I'd like to keep this.

Matron I don't know if that's possible. All possessions must go to the next of kin.

Wally I am his next of kin. Siamese twins weren't as close.

Matron The regulations are very strict about this sort of thing.

Wally You know my opinion of regulations.

Matron Fortunately your opinions don't change our rules. Even you must
see this has to be enforced or it might lead to all sorts of misappropriation.

Wally I think this is appropriate. Misappropriation! That's pinching. Are
you accusing me of pinching?

Matron I'm merely saying ——

Wally Potts and I have known each other nearly fifty years. We've been in
here four years. Shared the same room, the same food, at the same table.
I'd have done anything for Potts, as he would for me. So don't you accuse
me of thieving this ... ugly thing. It's a remembrance. He'd have given it,
given the chance. This is for four years.

Matron I know how you must be feeling.

Wally Good. Then you'll know why I'm hanging on to it.

Matron I'll see what I can do.

Wally I'm obliged. If the relative is that desperate for it I suggest an optician.
(*He leaves and shuts the door*)

The Lights come up in the room

Matron leaves her office

(*Entering the room*) Oh Christ! I'd forgotten about you. (*He returns to the
lobby*)

During the following, George finishes unpacking

Matron meets Wally in the lobby

Matron Mr Wallis?

Wally Matron, what's that bloke doing in my room?

Matron You will be sharing with him, for the time being.

Wally My friend isn't even cold yet.

Matron I'm very sorry, Mr Wallis. It was all rather quick.

Wally Quick! Who is he? Roger Bannister?

Matron The circumstances were rather exceptional.

Wally Don't I even get one night alone for my thoughts?

Matron I'm afraid that decision was taken by the owners. I did what I could.

Wally I'm sure you bent over backwards on my behalf.

Matron Consider where you are, Mr Wallis. This is a home for senior
citizens, we do anticipate death.

Wally And trample over its consequences.

Matron Some things are unavoidable. At least you have a secure home here.
There are others less fortunate.

Matron exits

Wally (*calling after her*) Potts is one of them. (*He returns to the room*)

George slides his case under his bed. Wally goes to the wardrobe but the chair is in his way

Did you put this chair here?
George Yes.
Wally Would you mind putting it back?
George I prefer it there.
Wally It's in my way.
George I don't see why you should need to be there. This is my side of the room.
Wally I wasn't aware it had sides. (*Pause*) I can't get to my place.

George can't bear fuss and moves the chair. Wally puts the umbrella on George's bed then runs his hand down the front of the wardrobe to the "right spot" — and bangs! A small panel flips open on the side. It hides a cubby hole with a bottle of whisky. He pours into the mug, replaces the whisky and shuts the panel. George replaces his umbrella. Wally throws his reefer jacket in the chair with George's jacket and sits. George reacts. Wally rises; George grabs his jacket and places it on his bed. He folds Wally's coat and places it on Wally's bed while Wally pulls the old trunk from under his bed, finds a packet of cigarettes in it and lights up. George sits. Wally sits in the chair facing and smokes, puffing rather than inhaling. George wafts the air

Seen someone you know?
George It's just the smoke.
Wally If all you can do is wave your hand about, get out in the garden and wave at the birds.
George I'm sorry.
Wally You're sorry. I'm sorry. I haven't smoked since I quit the sea. I came ashore and said, "That's it. New life; new habits". So don't stand there saying you're sorry when you should be someone else.
George Excuse me. I expect you would prefer to be alone.

George exits with his jacket

Wally (*sobbing*) Pottsy, what have you done? Where have you gone? You're part of me. How can you have gone when I'm still here? I won't have any more of this; you wouldn't want me to. (*He throws the cigarette in the basin and runs the tap*) I'm not giving up our medicine chest, mind. (*He raises the mug*) Good hiding-place of yours. Captain Bligh never suspected. Here's to you, Potts — and our good times. (*He drinks and sits*) But where are they now? I'll wake up soon. That's what'll happen. Wake up and find you're back. (*He cuddles the glass, sobbing gently*)

The Lights fade. Music. During the Black-out, Wally falls asleep in a chair

The Lights come up. It is two hours later

The music fades. An electronic tea bell sounds

May enters the lobby from the dining area carrying a piece of cake on a plate held at an acute angle; the cake falls off

George enters from the other corridor

May Oh firefly!
George Oh please, allow me. (*He puts the cake on the plate*) Would you like a fresh piece?
May A bit of dirt won't hurt. (*She blows the dust off*)
George Are they serving tea?
May (*heading for the bedroom*) If you've got the stamina to wait. Oh, and bring Wally a cup will you?
George Yes ... yes.

George exits

May enters the room and sings "Da-Da" to "The Hornpipe"

Wally (*waking with a start*) Potts?
May No. It's only me — "from over the sea, said Barnacle Bill the sailor." I brought you some cake.
Wally No tea?
May You're lucky to get cake.
Wally Madeira.
May Don't mention it. (*She sits*) You slept for hours. But you could do with some beauty sleep.
Wally Thank you, Fairy Godmother.
May You all right?
Wally I'll manage.
May Course you will but are you all right?
Wally I will be if you don't keep pestering me.
May Thank you, May, for bringing me this cake. Thank you, May, for showing some concern.
Wally Yes yes, slapped wrists, Granny. I'm all right. (*Pause*) I miss him, May.

May Course you do. Why don't you find out where they've laid him and tell him so. His spirit will be waiting to put you at your ease. (*She rises*)

Wally Don't go. Sit down; let's have a noggin.

May I can't. My daughter's coming.

Wally How is she?

May Makes me wish I'd never met her father.

Wally Maybe it was her upbringing.

May Well she didn't get it from me. Last week she took me to all the wrong places. All my shops had gone.

Wally They were there when I went out.

May The chemist was full of pictures of naked girls.

Wally For months now that chemist has been a porn shop.

May Then why did she take me there? What have I got to pawn at my age?

Wally I dread to think. (*He bites the cake — and wonders*) Did you put anything on this?

May (*a little guiltily*) Cinnamon. (*She leaves the room*)

Wally moves to sit on George's bed; he continues eating the cake

George enters the lobby with two cups of tea

May and George meet

What kept you? He needs that. Poor devil looks half dead himself.

George They ran out and had to make a refill.

May I've told them to buy a bigger pot. That thing wouldn't hold a dormouse. Mean old toadies.

May exits

George enters the room. Wally is sitting on George's bed eating the cake

George You were sound asleep when the bell went for tea.

Wally I wouldn't have heard Big Ben

George offers Wally a cup of tea

Very civil. (*He takes the cup and drinks*) Urgh! Did you put any sugar in this?

George One spoonful.

Wally Three spoonfuls. I like three spoonfuls.

George Surely you can't taste the tea.

Wally I hate tea. I like sweetness. (*He puts the cup down and eats*)

George That lady ...?

Wally May.

George May ... didn't look very safe with the cake but I see it arrived.

Wally She moves like a centipede with athlete's foot but she's got it up here (*he indicates his head*) — and a heart of gold.

George The food looks rather good here.

Wally Depends what you're used to.

George Not much lately. My mother was an excellent cook. Everything always meticulously served.

Wally We used to eat my mum's custard with a knife and fork. Still, doesn't matter what it looks like as long as it tastes good.

George On the contrary. Half the pleasure of food lives in the appearance.

Wally Where does tripe and onions fit in your scale of things? Looks as if it's still alive, and smells like an astronaut's jockstrap just after lift-off, but I could eat it four times a day. I love it.

George I prefer brightly-coloured food. Spring carrots, tropical fruit. The occasional rainbow trout.

Wally You'll love it here then. The food here resembles Blackpool illuminations only without the taste. Plenty of gravy, that's what I like. We had gravy on everything in the Merchant Navy. Even the bosun in heavy seas. (*He drops his cake*) Aw look at that! (*He picks it up*) Can't eat it now it's been on the floor. (*He drops the cake in the basket by the basin, leaving the plate and lots of crumbs on George's bed*)

George Excuse me asking, but was there any particular reason why you were eating your cake on my bed?

Wally Yes; I don't want a mess on my bed.

George brushes his bed

Matron enters her office and writes unobtrusively

Wally sluices his face noisily and hangs the towel on the tap. He puts Potts' mug on his shelf. Unhappy with this, he takes a picture from the wall and hangs the mug on the hook

There, Potts' pot, your new home.

George I'd like to say, Mr Wallis, how sorry I am about your friend. It must have been a great shock to you.

Wally If it's all the same I'd like to keep off the subject, especially with you. It's nothing personal but I can't help resenting you being here.

George I understand.

Wally Finished your tea?

George Oh, yes.

Wally Give us your cup.

George I'll take them back. I don't mind.

Wally Of course you don't but I want a word with Dr Crippen anyway. (*He leaves the room with the cups and knocks on Matron's door*)

George sits down to read a journal; the Lights fade on the room

Matron Come in.

Wally enters

Yes, Mr Wallis? What can I do for you?

Wally (*putting the cups on the desk*) I want to see Potts.

Matron I've explained about the funeral arrangements.

Wally No not the funeral. I don't fancy hanging about watching Nora the niece try to discover emotions. I want to see him — what do they call it? Ordinary people's lying in state.

Matron I don't think visits of that sort are a good idea.

Wally It's not an idea it's a necessity.

Matron takes a pill from a drawer and pours a glass of water

Matron Here Mr Wallis, take this.

Wally Very kind but I just had tea.

Matron It will calm you.

Wally I am calm.

Matron You've had a considerable shock. Indeed we are all very shocked.

Wally (*offering the water and pill to Matron*) Perhaps you should take it.

Matron You may think this is interference but seeing Mr Potterton — in that way — could be extremely upsetting for you.

Wally As opposed to the ecstatic way I feel now.

Matron You know very well what I mean.

Wally Just because we've all reached second childhood, Matron, you don't have to treat us like children.

Matron There are thirty-two people here to care for. It isn't always practical or possible to show individual affection or attention, however desirable that may be. I make no bones about not finding you the easiest person to get along with. However, there is nothing hypocritical in my concern. I am responsible.

Wally In the great scheme of things it's not one whit of importance if you don't like me and I don't give a sailor's shilling for you. This is an old people's home and nature in its infinite bloody-mindedness has decreed me old and this my home. The price I pay for this little bit of comfort is to live under your divine guidance but that should not take away my right to pay my respects to my friend, nor should you make me feel guilty or sick because I want to.

Matron (*after a pause*) Very well. I will telephone and see what arrangements can be made.

Wally I'm much obliged. (*He heads for the exit*)

Matron If you take the pill.

Wally (*grumbling*) Oh ... (*He pops the pill into his mouth and has a gulp of water*)

Matron Thank you. Now, is there anything else I can do for you?

Wally What I want is not within your giving. (*He goes out and shuts the door. He spits the pill into his hand, throws it in the air and kicks it away*)

Matron comes out of her office with the cups

Matron Mr Wallis.

Wally (*thinking he's been caught*) Matron.

Matron Why not pay your respects at morning service tomorrow? It would be nice to see you there.

Wally God and I have a mutual lack of communication.

Matron I shall be giving a small commemoration service.

Wally Don't hold back on my account.

Matron You might benefit by letting the bond of Christianity help you.

Wally I doubt it and Potts would hate such devotion.

Matron Don't begrudge a shared mourning amongst the faithful. Mr Potterton was a friend to us all.

Wally Even the grim reaper makes mistakes.

Matron exits towards the dining area

The Lights come up. Wally enters the room and sniffs the flowers

Wally Did you bring these?

George No. Matron.

Wally Probably from the hospital.

George She said they were from the crematorium.

Wally That woman has a gift for diplomacy. (*He kicks off his deck-shoes, gets into bed and pulls the covers over his head*)

George watches uncertainly

The Lights fade. During the Black-out, George neatens his side of the room

Sunday. Peals of church bells segue into electronic church bells as the Lights come up. George straightens his tie and puts on his jacket. Wally lies in a shambolic heap

May enters from the dining-room with a plate of toast

Matron comes from her office and May hears her door shut. Matron heads for the room

George leaves the room

May (*thrusting the plate at George*) Give this to Wally, will you, or I shall miss my place in the pew.
George Yes. Of course.

May exits

George returns to the room. Matron nears

Mr Wallis? Mr Wallis. (*He nudges Wally*)
Wally (*waking*) It's not my watch.
George May has sneaked you out some toast.

Matron knocks and breezes into the room

Matron Everyone decent? Major Fairbrother, what are you doing with that toast? I made it clear about food in the room.
George Yes, but ——
Matron No buts. Black mark. (*She whisks the plate from his hand*)

Wally gleefully slaps his own wrist

Up, up, up, Mr Wallis. You've been allowed a special lie-in. Don't take advantage.
Wally My special lie-in is because you drugged me.
Matron Don't ramble. Get up. (*She pulls his bedclothes*)
Wally (*grabbing the bedclothes*) Hey hey! Leave my bedclothes alone. You don't know what state I'm in under here.
Matron Unfortunately I'm all too familiar with under there.
Wally I don't want to get up.
Matron Come along.
Wally I shouldn't have to get up on a Sunday.
Matron It's the Lord's day and He wants you up.
Wally I can't think why.
Matron Neither can I but that's His mystery. I hope you're not going to defy me, Mr Wallis?
Wally Yes, Matron.

Matron Then Nurse Wiggins will be sent to you.
Wally No, Matron. (*He rises quickly*)
Matron Church in the dining-room at eleven, Major.
George Yes, Matron.

Matron exits with the toast

Wally puts on his shoes

Who is Nurse Wiggins?
Wally Wiggins is the Mafia in size forty-two. She had a choice between being a nurse or playing for the All Blacks. (*He does a brief Haka*) She has my deepest respect. What's all this Major stuff?
George I was a regular soldier.
Wally That explains a lot. (*He sluices his face*)

Electronic bells peal

George I'd better be off.
Wally Have you a penny for the plate — Major?

George exits to the dining area

Well Potts, I slept the sleep of the dead. But only you'd know about that. It may have soothed the savage beast — but where do we go from here, eh?

He opens the door and from the dining area the congregation is heard singing the end of a hymn accompanied by a harmonium

Congregation (*off: singing*) Oh hear us when we cry to thee
                                    For those in peril on the sea.
Wally What do they know about peril on the sea?
Congregation (*off*) A — men.
Matron (*off*) According to Revelations, "And the sea gave up the dead which were in it" ——
Wally (*to himself*) Ah shut up.
Matron (*off*) — "and they were judged every man according to his works."
Wally Pack it in.
Matron (*off*) Mr Potterton will be judged as a man who ——
Wally Don't mention Potts' name. He was my friend.

During Matron's next speech Wally bursts out of the room and charges across the lobby

Matron (*off*) — understood the Christian way. He lived in God's eye and
his reward was a rich, fulfilling ——
Wally Stop this sham! Stop it! Stop it!

*Wally exits to the dining area. The congregation is disrupted. We hear the
babble of many overlapping voices including :*

Matron (*off*) Mr Wallis! What do you think you're doing?
Wally (*off*) Potts lived by the laws of nature. Not this.
Matron (*off*) Control yourself.
Wally (*off*) This is a sham.
George (*off*) How dare you interrupt this service.
May (*off*) Go back, Wally. You shouldn't be here.
George (*off*) This service is for your friend.
Wally (*off*) He'd have hated this.
Matron (*off*) You've gone too far this time.
May (*off*) God only takes because he loves.
Wally (*off*) It's a pity he didn't love somebody else.
Matron (*off*) Mrs Harris — "What a Friend We Have In Jesus."

The harmonium starts. The congregation sings raggedly

Matron pulls Wally on from the dining area

Wally (*calling off behind him*) Don't sing in Potts' name. He was my friend.
I'll put him to rest.
Matron I suppose you're pleased with your selfish display? Disturbing our
penance like that. Half the congregation think they're at a revivalist
meeting. Made yourself rather over-excited, haven't you?
Wally For Christ's sake, woman, I'm not losing my marbles.
Matron That remains to be seen. Will you be quiet? Or need I administer to
you?
Wally When can I see Potts?
Matron Are you going to be quiet?
Wally When?
Matron Tomorrow morning. At eleven. Until then I want you on your best
behaviour.

Wally exits

The hymn ends untidily

And start treating Major Fairbrother decently. He is now a resident and
likely to remain so.

Matron follows Wally off

May and George enter from the dining-room

May Well, that service should have made the Good Lord sit up and listen.
George Is it always that lively?
May Unfortunately not.
George Thank heaven for that.
May Don't judge Wally too harshly, under his present circumstances.
George I wish I'd been made aware of his circumstances before I moved in.
May No matter what either of you feel there's little you can do about it.
George No. Besides I wouldn't want to go back. I've been sharing with three others in temporary accommodation since my wife died. "A room with mildew" I called it. A play on the title of the book, you see.
May Oh? Oh yes. Very good.
George I thought I was paying for a single room here, but there's a delay, it seems.
May (*giggling*) Mr Gomez and the ceiling.
George Yes. That's right. Still I imagine it will be easier sharing with one than three.
May I wouldn't bank on it.
George I got used to a certain amount of discomfort in the army.
May I had you down for an army man. Something about the carriage.
George The family business, you might say. My father commanded the regiment. He was a born leader. Died, as I think he would have wanted, in battle. The Normandy landings.
May Poor soul.
George They gave him a posthumous DSO.
May Fancy.
George I'd been commissioned a couple of years before. Although I don't delude myself that my contribution was particularly distinguished, I hope it was respected.
May I'm sure it was. We were in dresses.
George Dresses?
May My hubby and I. Good quality frocks for the chain store market. We were making ethnic when it was still called foreign. My Harold knew just what women wanted. I carried on after he'd gone, until my second fall. My daughter took me in. Do you have children?
George (*after a beat*) Unfortunately no.
May Take my tip, if you ever get round to it: never educate them above your station. They become ashamed of you. I wasn't having that, so I came in here.
George I see.
May Have you settled in to a particular seat for your meals yet?

George Matron has a misplaced idea I enjoy crossword puzzles. So she's put me with Mr Amos. He never stops giving me clues.

May You're very welcome to join my table.

George That's most kind.

May It's full of dreadful old fogeys.

George I'll attempt a little light relief.

May Thank you.

George Is there a decent spot of lunch here on Sundays?

May A culinary delight. Fifty ways to ruin chicken.

They laugh. May looks at George cheekily. Music

May exits jauntily

George remains, slightly bemused

The Lights cross-fade to an evening setting

George enters the room and sees the mess

George Oh my God! (*He removes his jacket, draws the curtains and makes Wally's bed with army precision. He folds Wally's coat and places it on the end of his bed with his hat. He places his chair at the end of his bed and Wally's to one side. He hangs Wally's towel on a hook by the basin and starts to wash his hands*)

The music fades

Wally enters. During the following he sits on the coat on his bed

I shan't be a moment. Do you want the basin?

Wally No. Apart from peeing in it twice a day I hardly use the thing.

George Oh I say.

Wally Just a little joke, old son. Don't panic. I shared a cabin once with a bloke called Fairbrother. We sank together in 1952. We abandoned ship and a lifeboat fell right on top of him.

George How terrible.

Wally Gave him a splitting headache.

George goes to the wardrobe

What I'm saying is this: we none of us know what's going to happen next. Life chops and changes more often than a rabbi at a circumcision, so we may as well get on as fall out.

George I couldn't agree more. (*He puts his jacket on a hanger*)

Wally I'm always called Wally. You know, as in Wally Wallis, Jimmy James, Chalky White. (*Pause*) What about you?

George I find George acceptable.

Wally You're not gay are you, George?

George Gay?

Wally Don't worry. I've a liberal attitude to other people's way of life but you seem a bit ... prim.

George I'm tidy not prim. The army taught me the value of order. (*He hangs his jacket in the wardrobe and puts on his dressing-gown*)

Wally Oh well then, Colonel ...

George Major.

Wally Major.

George Thank you. How do I know you're not gay?

Wally You don't, Colonel, but at my age it won't make any difference.

George I find your snap judgement of my character highly offensive.

Wally I didn't mean to offend you. It's good to sort these things out at the start so we know where we are.

George I know where I am. Sharing a room with you. A situation which neither of us would have chosen and which hopefully will not last long. While it does I ask you to respect my privacy, as far as our circumstances permit, and I undertake to respect yours.

Wally What do you propose? A vow of silence?

George No of course not. Merely that we should not feel obliged to talk ... for talking's sake.

Wally I'm not afraid of words or the emotions they can conjure up. To me talk's talk.

George I am probably influenced by my father, who incidentally *was* a colonel. He didn't hold with frivolous chat, so a great many topics were taboo in our household which no doubt in other homes were part of everyday conversation.

Wally When you've been dragged up by the seat of your pants you see the world from a different angle.

George No doubt. (*He offers Wally his hand*)

They shake hands. George gets his slippers and as they talk he removes his shoes, puts trees in them and puts them by the chest of drawers

Do you remember that poster in the war: "Careless talk costs lives"?

Wally What about it?

George My father applied it in peacetime as well. In his view careless talk undermined authority and produced chaos.

Wally I like chaos — it's natural.

George I hope you don't mind, I put a bit of order into yours.

Wally I don't bother about my surroundings much. It's what you do in life, not how you display things.

George All the same I'm surprised you didn't build up a collection of souvenirs from your time at sea.

Wally I did. But Potts said things like that were just sand round the oasis. Living by memories he called it. And he was right. Mind you, I kept it all. Stuffed it away in the trunk out of sight.

George When the present is empty the past can be a great comfort.

Wally The past is for museums. People are for today. Potts thought it was called the past for a damn good reason, so you don't have to live with it. Mind you his memory was shorter than the Italian Book of War Heroes. He said he wouldn't remember his wife if she fell in through the door with divorce papers. They'd been separated for forty-two years, and he couldn't decide if that was grounds for desertion or cruelty.

George I lost my wife a year ago. That's why I'm here.

Wally Ran off with another bloke, did she?

George No. Died.

Wally Oh, departed with Jesus.

George She died of alcohol poisoning.

Wally Oh what a way to go!

George I find that remark in the worst possible taste.

Wally (*bowing*) Oh *tuan*, I'm sorry. I know, I can lap waves. *Bwana mkubwa*. Listen Colonel, you mustn't be upset by my sailor's humour. A bit coarse I grant you but it might be all we have between us.

George Yes, well I've always had difficulty laughing at myself or indeed others. I'm no doubt the poorer because of it.

Wally Some of my best nights have been spent with people with no more in common than laughter. Mind you, alcohol is a great interpreter.

George I gave up drink in order to help Marjorie with her problem.

Wally But it didn't?

George No. My fault in a way, I suppose.

Wally What happened?

George Well, Marjorie came from a well-heeled county family and when I married her after the war I couldn't find a job in civvy street to support her in the way to which she was accustomed. My mother wanted a soldier in the family and persuaded me to take a regular commission in my late father's regiment. So I took the bride off to Malaya, slap into the Communist emergency. Marjorie was terrified of the jungle and terrified of the insurgents. I was away a lot and she started drinking.

Wally You can't blame her.

George I don't. Our next posting was to Kenya, which was better at first. Until the Mau Mau business started up and made things even worse. So I packed her off home. When I was eventually offered command of my battalion, Marjorie said, "You must choose between me and your bloody regiment". So I chose her. Have you ever married?

Wally Turn it up! I thought about it once and was ill for a week. Lovely girl, mind. Fabulous cook and a body to keep us both warm in winter. I only asked her because I didn't think she'd say yes. When she did I signed on for a long, slow, round-the-world job and met up with Potts. A long time. (*Pause*) Reminds me: two Chelsea Pensioners sitting on a bench and a pretty girl walks by like that. And one says to the other, "'Ere, d'you remember that stuff they used to put in our tea during the war to stop us feeling sexy?" And the other one says, "Yeah. What about it?" And the first one says, "I think mine's just beginning to work." (*He laughs*)

George (*not laughing*) I don't think I ever tried that.

Wally I don't think you'd need to. Nutburger probably did for you. (*He pulls his trunk out*)

George Oh here we go; the vegetarian jokes. If you have any more get them over and done with now. Purge yourself.

Wally Rissoles. (*He opens the lid of the trunk; the opening faces away from the audience*)

George Yes, I've heard them all. As you can see I do not talk like a swede or need a leek. Nor do I have Jesus sandals or carry a haversack.

Wally lifts a shrunken head out of the trunk and lobs it at George

Wally Ever seen one of those?

George Urgh!

Wally It's all right — it's quite dead. I got it thirty years ago in South America. Bloke told me it was the head of an escaped Nazi. Doesn't look too impressive.

George Perhaps he was only a little Nazi.

Wally Made you jump.

George It was the unexpected. I'm not used to handling heads.

Wally Back in the box, Fritz. (*He puts the head in the trunk but makes it escape along the lid with a ventriloquist's "Heil Hitler. Heil Hitler"*) Get back. Get back. (*He throws the head inside the trunk and slams the lid*) You see that? He nearly escaped again. (*He makes the trunk shake*) "Heil Hitler". Shut up. "Heil Hitler". I told you, he shot himself. (*He takes out the head again*) I better cover his ears up. (*He does so*) He's still writing to Eva Braun. (*He puts the head back and takes out a small electric stove*) From within this cornucopia — hey presto! The *Mighty Little Wizard* electric stove. (*He puts the stove on the floor near his bed and uncoils the lead*) The Indian plug trick. (*Making Indian rope trick sounds he balances the plug upright before plugging it in*) There we are. Oh George, if you wouldn't mind opening the window.

George But it's chilly.

Wally Must have fresh air, Colonel.

George opens the window and puts on his overcoat

Now the pan. *Voilà!* (*He takes a frying pan from the chest of drawers and wipes it round with an item of underwear*) Remember to always keep your frying pan in with your smalls. Matron is reluctant to trespass in a bloke's undies. (*He checks the stove is heating and puts on the pan*) See that pan? I bought that in the United States. Pan American. Now ... (*He removes George's umbrella from the side of the wardrobe again, grumbling as he does so*) Oil. (*He finds another "spot" on the wardrobe and bangs it. A second panel opens in the side. Wally takes out a bottle of oil and pours some in the pan*) Oil — or as the French say *l'huile*. (*He sings*) "Every little breeze seems to whisper *l'huile*". (*He replaces the container in the wardrobe*) Now George, what did you do with my steak?

George (*getting the steak from the top of the wardrobe*) I hope you're not going to cook that.

Wally It's too late to take it to market.

George Not in here?

Wally No George, in the wardrobe.

George But Matron is adamant about food in the room.

Wally I know but I like to spend my little bit of money on things that upset her. It gives the meat added flavour. (*He unwraps the steak and throws the paper on to the wardrobe on to George's hat*)

George tidies up and re-hangs his umbrella

Now the trick is to spread it out like they do in restaurants, so they can give you a smaller portion of peas. Find a nice hard surface like that. (*He taps the chest of drawers and puts the unwrapped steak on top*) Cover it for hygiene. (*He takes a red spotted hanky from his pocket and lays it over the steak*) Find a good solid object — (*he grabs one of George's smart shoes*) — and tenderize! (*He bashes the steak with the shoe*)

George That's my shoe.

Wally I'm only using the heel. (*Bash*)

George You can't have it.

Wally I need to bash the steak.

George Use one of your own shoes.

Wally They bounce. (*Bash*)

George Stop it. No. Stop that. (*He pulls Wally away*)

Wally Never stand between a man and his gastric juices.

George (*wrestling with Wally over his shoe*) Stop this carnage of my Oxfords. (*He gets the shoe away from Wally*) These shoes weren't made for laying waste to cattle.

Wally Before you bought them they were cattle.

George Look at it. Filthy. Blood all over the heel.

Wally That heel does a very nice steak. (*He holds up the steak, checks the pan and sits on the edge of his bed to cook*)

George sits as far away as possible

The secret of cooking steak is to have the pan desert hot. (*He drops in the steak. It must sizzle!*) I love that sound. Have you never liked meat? (*He reaches under his bed and brings out a chamber pot containing herbs and condiments which he shakes over the steak. He gets a spatula and meat fork from the trunk which he uses as they talk*) Oh, come on, George, don't be in a huff over a shoe. You should be pleased. I always used Potts' shoe before. Talk to me.

George My father put me off red meat. He had a passion for steak. Mother would drop it in the pan — tssst! Done. When he cut into it it would haemorrhage. Then he'd eat it without chewing, like a seagull. By the time I was eighteen I could only face vegetables. Aren't you afraid this smell will give you away?

Wally That's why you opened the window. Don't fuss.

George I don't want to get into any more trouble on my first weekend.

Wally Quite right. Save it up till next weekend.

George Supposing you're caught?

Wally I plead senility. Matron would have a dark blue fit if she caught me with a stove in the room but the thought of her having one only encourages me. Sure you wouldn't like some?

George I already feel like an accessory. I might take a detective novel to the lounge for a quiet read.

Wally Take something from my library if you like.

George (*reading*) Mutiny on the Bounty. Mr Midshipman Hornblower. The Cruel Sea. Janes' Fighting Ships.

Wally I've only looked at the pictures in that one.

George All marine subjects. Have you read many books about the sea?

Wally Yes. All three.

George Just these three?

Wally Well I like those.

George You've not liked any other books?

Wally I haven't read any other books. With my education I got Z minus for the three Rs and A plus for anything behind the bike shed.

George Who taught you to read?

Wally A cabin steward I once bunked with. Right Communist he was. Started me off with *Mutiny on the Bounty*. I think he was hoping to convert me. He might have, only it took two and a half years to get to the end. By the time I finished I'd forgotten what the mutiny was about. After four years I'd read one book twice; I was hooked.

George At that pace three books would be as much as one could appreciate.

Wally Course I'm faster now.

George Wouldn't you like to read something else?

Wally No, I'm getting used to where the words are now. Watch this. I'm going to turn this steak with the quickest flip in history. (*He taps the pan with the spatula and pretends to throw the steak high in the air*)

George isn't fooled — but plays the game

Would you like to see it again? (*He turns the steak*)

George This rather reminds me of camping.

Wally Dib dob dib. Rain on your woggle and insects up the leg of your little shorts.

George I was a most enthusiastic Scout.

Wally I had a feeling you would be.

George I had badges all up my arm. Summers under canvas. Happy days. I owe a great deal to the Scout movement; it broadened my outlook. Do you cook in here regularly?

Wally Only at weekends. (*In a phoney French accent*) I am wern erve ze world's great smerll sterve chefs. Look at that. Perfectly cooked.

George In that case I will unplug this thing. (*He does*) From tomorrow I shall wear gloves. I don't want my fingerprints all over the illegal.

Wally Self-preservation. Highly commendable. (*He goes to the wardrobe and finds the umbrella in his way again! He grabs it and rages at it indecipherably but loudly, then lays it on George's bed*) There's not a lot you can say to an umbrella. Now — bread. (*He finds a third "spot" on the front of the wardrobe and bangs. Another panel flips open and he removes two slices of bread and makes a sandwich with the steak*) There. Old folks' home cooking. Sure you don't want some? Me and Potts used to share.

George No. Thank you.

Wally (*biting*) Mmm. Bloody good bit of steak this.

George I'm glad it was worth the effort.

Wally You don't know what you're missing. (*He puts the sandwich on the bed as he puts on his coat and hat*) Well George, I can see you love it here so I'm off to the pub. If you feel lured by the Song of the Sirens take no notice. It's Mrs Achensmith's hearing aid picking up Radio One. (*He picks up the steak and Potts' mug*) Come on Potts' pot — say hallo to the landlord. (*He goes to the window*) Matron told me to be on my best behaviour, so I might be back before the milk wagon churns up Bournvita Boulevard.

George May I close the window now?

Wally For goodness sake no! It's my only access and at my age damp seeps quickly into vital parts. (*He climbs out of the window*)

George What about these things?

Wally (*looking in thorugh the window*) I'll clear them up when I get back.

George Won't Matron find them?

Wally I don't know, George — but if she does and you're still here, you won't half cop it.

Wally exits

Music. George looks at the mess and goes to tidy up

CURTAIN

ACT II

Monday. It is sunny

The lobby is now set as the Chapel of Rest, with a coffin downstage (or, when needed, a lighting effect can suggest the coffin)

All the furniture in the bedroom is initialled with "G" or "W". White tape runs down the centre from the wardrobe and around both beds providing narrow paths inside and one outside from door to basin

When the CURTAIN *rises, George, in his shirtsleeves, is completing his division of the room by sticking a strip of tape from the roll in his hand to the carpet. He firms it with his foot. He adjusts his bedside cabinet and sees a note on the floor addressed to Wally. He is about to put it on his bed but looks at it again*

May enters

George hides the note

May Morning, George.
George Oh, good-morning, May.
May Wally gone, has he?
George About an hour ago.
May I shall probably miss my own funeral.
George I'll see you get there. Oh — no. I don't mean ——
May Are you decorating?
George Just having a little change around.
May Oh yes?
George I'm afraid the situation between Mr Wallis and myself has reached breaking point.
May Consider his predicament.
George I do, but our ways of looking at things are quite irreconcilable.
May I do love the way you talk.
George Oh, thank you. So I wrestled with the problem of our co-habitation and came up with this brilliant idea. Divide the room in two.
May Does Wally know?
George Not exactly. But when it's fully marked out I think he'll find it acceptable.

May Do you?
George It just creates a little order.
May Order's a red rag to him.
George It's a necessity to me. May — would you mind?
May Eh?
George Would you put your stick on the end there?

George puts the roll of tape on the floor, May plonks her stick on the tape and George pulls out a last strip

There. Now isn't that much better? Surely Mr Wallis will appreciate this is the only possible solution.
May No George, he won't appreciate this one little bit. But I can't wait till he comes back and sees it. (*She laughs*)

The Lights fade to Black-out

During the following, George puts his jacket on and tidies the room

The Chapel of Rest. (*For alternative scene, see p. 53*)

Quiet organ music plays

Wally enters upstage of the coffin, his face lit with a sepulchral glow pinpointing the private world of respect in which the living face the dead. He pulls off his hat

The music fades out

Wally Hallo, Pottsy. They've made you look very good, old friend. Better than you did in life. I don't suppose that old body of yours can feel much now. Your pain has gone. Mine's just beginning. I know — don't be morbid. Death is only God's way of telling you to "sod off". Everyone says nice things about you. Matron clearly wishes I was in your place. Nurse Wiggins shook my hand and nearly dislocated my thumb. She's going to carry the coffin — by herself. Smile, Potts. Talk to me once more. Oh, Potts, we had the whole world living in our minds, now it's deserted. Is it too late to talk about love? I know you loved everyone, that was your gift to life, but you even made me feel loved, nobody's done that before: I didn't know how to respond. My love's always been for nature's things: the sea, open sky, the cry of the seagulls. I never knew about love for people. Your way. If it's not too late — I'd like to say I love you. I don't know how, Potts, but somehow I'll find a way of taking you with me. Perhaps that will give me the strength to carry on. (*He reaches out as if touching Potts' head*) Goodbye, old friend. My only other life.

The music fades up

Wally exits

The Lights fade to Black-out, then come up on the bedroom and corridor

The music becomes a military march from George's cassette/radio. George marches with precision up and down the tape and into the corridor

Matron enters the corridor and meets George

George salutes, becomes flustered and shuts the bedroom door. The music fades into the background

George Sorry — just my recording of the Trooping.
Matron Oh, I'm all in favour of keep fit. Is Mr Wallis back yet?
George I haven't seen him, Matron.
Matron I always worry about people's reactions after they've visited a Chapel of Rest. The deceased can take on an unnatural existence in a coffin.
George Yes. I went to say goodbye to my wife in the Chapel of Rest. A number of things had been left unsaid during her final years. The visit was not a success.
Matron I'm sorry.
George Marjorie had developed an effortless way of winning an argument. I shouldn't have gone. I knew how she hated unexpected visitors.
Matron How strange, I always prefer the unexpected ones to those I know are coming. Coffee in the dining-room, Major.
George Thank you. (*He turns, salutes, realizes*) Oh ... er ...

They exit

During the next scene the Chapel of Rest set is struck and the garden set is put in place

Wally enters. He opens the door to the room and the music gets louder. He angrily flicks the music off

Wally This is a forward mess deck, not Wellington Barracks. Oh Potts. (*He notices the divisions in the room*) What the ...

George enters the room with a cup of coffee

What the hell is this?
George Coffee.

Wally Don't try it on old son. What's all this bloody white tape? It isn't Whitehall.

George That's red tape.

Wally You're heading for a red nose you are. What's this stuck all over my floor?

George It's our floor and it's to denote our areas.

Wally I'll denote your area. (*He discards his hat and coat and puts up his fists*)

George Don't threaten me or I shall be forced to retaliate.

Wally threatens George

I am trained in unarmed combat. (*The cup shakes on the saucer*)

Wally Your hand's shaking.

George In spite of my calling I have an innate abhorrence of violence. I've seen too much. The thought of it can make me physically sick.

Wally Then don't drink your coffee. This carpet's in enough mess as it is.

George I know you think of me as a usurper.

Wally Bollocks.

George I beg your pardon?

Wally It's an old naval expression meaning bollocks.

George I was hoping we could discuss this rationally.

Wally I can't talk rationally with a nutcase.

George Try to see it from my point of view.

Wally What about my view — of my room.

George It is also my room.

Wally I was here first.

George I've allowed for that. You have the bigger half.

Wally What do you mean half? A vole would get claustrophobia.

George This tape is to define our borders.

Wally Fine. You stick to your half and I'll carry on as before.

George No, no, that just won't work.

Wally It worked perfectly well before you came.

George Just take a moment and you'll see it's much better organized. For instance we both obviously still use the entire basin.

Wally Oh good. I don't just get the cold tap.

George But my flannel is on one side and yours will be on the other.

Wally I don't use a flannel. My hands are good enough for those awkward little places.

George We each have our own things in our own area. One side of the wardrobe; one cabinet; our own chair.

Wally Suppose I don't like that chair.

George They're the same.

Wally No they're not. This one's good for forty winks. But you have to stay awake in that one or it cricks your back.

George Just try it for a week.

Wally I'm not having a cricked back for a week. You have that chair.

George I've labelled them.

Wally I can't read.

George Oh all right, all right I'll change them. I don't mind. (*He swaps the chairs and initials*) You really will find it much more agreeable knowing the whereabouts of your own things.

Wally No it won't. Where's the surprise in that? (*He points at the chest of drawers*) And what's this "W" stand for? Woollies?

George No — Wallis. So we don't mix up our clothes.

Wally I've only got a duffle coat and a bobble hat.

George But you do tend to spread them about.

Wally I'll spread you about.

George At least think about it!

Wally sits in the pose of Rodin's "Thinker" and ... thinks

Wally (*rising*) Right. I've thought. I liked it the way it was.

George Where are you going?

Wally Arbitration.

George It was Matron who authorized the changes.

Wally That woman has never liked me.

George This is a very confined space and it's vital we reconcile our points of view. Yours outgoing, open. Mine needing definition and borders. We want a home from home here, not some rubbish tip.

Wally You'll think a rubbish tip is savoury by the time I've finished. If you want division in your life you're about to start lessons from a master. (*He throws his hat at George's feet*) Your timing is about as handy as the lookout on the *Titanic*.

Wally exits

George kicks the hat over the line then picks it up and throws it on Wally's bed

The Lights fade on him. Music. The Lights come up on the garden

May sits asleep on a rustic bench in front of a pretty, flower-covered trellis or wall

The music fades

Matron enters with a pillow

Matron Come along, May.

She pushes May forward, puts the pillow at her back and pulls her on to it

There, everything better now?
May (*sweetly*) Yes thank you, Matron.

Matron moves away

(*Pulling a face*) Won't even let you fart in this place. (*She falls asleep during the following*)

Wally enters

Matron Ah, Mr Wallis. Was everything all right this morning? You didn't find it too upsetting?
Wally It helped.
Matron Oh. I'm glad.
Wally Pottsy looked better than new. Thank you.
Matron Well ... (*She gestures as if it was nothing*)
Wally That bloke in my room has changed everything round.
Matron Yes.
Wally He says you gave him permission.
Matron It seemed churlish to dampen his enthusiasm.
Wally What about me?
Matron I thought it would be less disturbing to move things while you were out.
Wally There's a lot gets moved while I'm out.
Matron I'm happy Major Fairbrother is amiable and prepared to enter into the spirit of things here.
Wally I didn't know it was a holiday camp. (*He does a couple of mini star jumps*)
Matron Please don't make a fuss about this.
Wally How would you like it if I altered your home while you were out?
Matron I often move the furniture in my flat. It helps take the mind off one's problems.
Wally I'm looking at my problem.
Matron Wishing to be blunt, Mr Wallis, old age is sometimes a confusion in itself. I am here to achieve clarity and order. People set in old ways have to become set in new ways. My ways. Like it or not, I am the final arbiter. Lunch in fifteen minutes.

She exits

Wally (*saluting*) *Jawohl, Herr Gruppenfuhrer.* (*He sees May sleeping, picks a flower then creeps behind her and covers her eyes with his hands*)

May Who's that?

Wally Buffalo Bill.

May Don't shoot! I'm a defenceless old woman.

Wally You defenceless? Moby Dick wouldn't attack you. I brought you a flower. (*He sits beside her and offers the flower*)

May Bit sentimental for you.

Wally I am sentimental.

May Mental more like. (*She smells the flower*) It smells of cat.

Wally I picked that one specially.

May Thank you.

Wally 'Ere, d'you know what the bloke George has gone and done? Divided up the room with tape. The carpet looks like a running track.

May I told him you wouldn't like it.

Wally I nearly wrapped him up in his tape and stuck both ends up his — jumper.

May Why wrestle with temptation?

Wally It's bad enough having to share with someone else but to be given a loony.

May How do you know I'm not a loony?

Wally I only have to share a bench with you.

May I'm a rather sorry sort of loony. I only smell up one nostril. See through one eye. Hear in one ear. Now, would you believe, Matron wants me to use a walking frame. I flatly refuse to go around supported by bits of scaffolding. I want a say in the decline of my dignity. Perhaps your Potts had the right idea. Got out while he was still ahead.

Wally This isn't like you, May.

May Sometimes I think the only thing holding me together is my elastic stockings. I can still read with a magnifier yet that silly Cynthia insists on reading me the paper every morning. I know I'm going senile 'cos I put up with it. God knows what paper she reads but it goes on and on about sex as if it's just been discovered. My hubby and I had a very good sex life long before it was popular. He dropped dead when he was sixty-four. It went downhill after that. I was just nudging sixty and still raring to go.

Wally We should have met then. I was just coming up to my prime. Sadly the youthful Adonis you see before you now could crumble to dust waiting for afternoon tea.

May Not you, Wally. You won't start dying before your time. Some of them come in here, and because they're here, start to believe they've had it. They don't have to do anything, so they do less and less until half of them give up doing at all. They accept that the status quo is idleness. I hate the pointlessness of that existence; it might rub off on me.

Wally Let's run away together before it's too late.

May Ooh, Gretna Green.

Wally I'll get you a pair of roller skates and push you.

May When I was nine I ran away on roller skates. Got six miles and half the ball bearings fell out. Never went on skates again.

Wally I ran away once, for keeps. I was always playing truant from school. Kept wanting to live it not hear about it. One day I put my hand up in class to go to the lavvy and I never went back. They must have thought I had terrible constipation. I scribbled a note on the kitchen table, took the rent money from the tea caddy and had my thirteenth birthday crossing the equator.

May You should go and see if the equator's still there.

Wally Potts and I talked about it all the time. But you know me, that was — talk. Besides, when Potts was here I figured I was kitted out for the duration.

May The sea was a good friend to you.

Wally I hear she's been going out with other sailors.

May But she always comes back in.

Wally I'm not the same, May. Part of me's gone and can't be replaced. A friendship like ours was once in a lifetime.

May What we need is a daring escape plan to make us feel good.

Wally We'll bribe Wiggins to create a diversion.

May Or set fire to the curtains like Mrs Pankurst did.

Wally No: we'll just walk out dressed up as nurses.

May You haven't got the legs for it.

George enters the garden with the note

We could ask George.

Wally George hasn't the legs for it.

May For an escape plan.

Wally He couldn't plan breakfast.

May He's writing a detective story.

Wally He pinches it all from other books.

May George is looking at you.

Wally I can't think why. We're not speaking.

May Wally says you're not speaking.

George I have a message for him.

May George says he has a message for you.

Wally What is it?

May Wally wants to know what it is?

George passes the note to May who passes it to Wally who passes it back to May

Wally You read it.
May I haven't got my magnifier. (*She passes the note to George*)
George Will that be all right?
May George says will that be all right?

Wally shrugs to May who shrugs to George

George I found it on the floor when I was taping the room. It says "To Wally" on the outside. (*He opens the note. Reading*) "I'm becalmed, old friend. Can't see the breeze getting back into my sails. When the worst has happened make sure you give my body to the sea as she gave to me all my life. I love you." And there's a — kiss. (*He holds the note out*)

May takes the note and looks at the "kiss", then passes it to Wally. He studies the note

Wally That's not a kiss, that's his signature.

May laughs; George smiles with relief

Potts could write perfectly well but it gave him pleasure to make his mark rather than sign his name.
May George. (*She jerks her head*)

George looks. May jerks her head again

George exits

Wally, I want to give you something.
Wally Oh no, May, you've given me enough.
May This is something practical. (*She removes a gold locket on a chain from her neck*) Here.
Wally I can't take this.
May You're not having it. Take that locket off the chain.

He does

Now give that to me.

He offers both the chain and the locket to May

No, the locket.

He hands her the locket

(*Trying to open it*) Oh my thumbs are all fingers. You do it.

He opens the locket upside down

That's my hubby. My "Little Squirrel".
Wally You never showed me this before. Why's he standing on his head?

May turns the locket the right way up

May I'll give you such a doe-boy.
Wally When was this taken?
May Yonks ago. Before the camera. Give it back.
Wally (*holding on to the locket*) Surely this other picture is of a film star. This girl is beautiful.
May I was beautiful.
Wally Queen of the May all year round, eh? Now I know why you had such a good time.
May What do you mean?
Wally You know what I mean.
May That's all I've got, Wally. You and a couple of old photographs no bigger than a penny stamp. (*Pause*) I want you to take the chain.
Wally I can't take this chain. The locket will keep dropping down into your knickers.
May Talk about looking a gift horse ——
Wally May, as if I can take this. It's lovely but I can't take it.
May It isn't for you — as such. It's for me. I'm not going anywhere now. (*She touches her head*) But I can up here. And you can go anywhere you like. Why not? What's to keep you here now? Why shouldn't you go swimming again in the Indian Ocean? Or shopping again in Hong Kong harbour? Or laying your head under a palm tree and having a coconut fall on it, which would be a fitting end. Any of those things you told me about. So, I want you to take that chain and sell it. It's solid gold so you'll get plenty for it. My "Little Squirrel" was clever with money. Go on, Wally: take it, sell it and go. But — I want picture postcards, at least twice a week, until the money runs out.
Wally (*bursting out laughing and hugging her*) Oh, May.
May You can stop all this.
Wally No I can't. You're a cracker.
May I want big postcards mind.
Wally Kingsize.
May My mind is full of memories, Wally. Absolutely crammed. But I'm going to push something out — to always have a memory of you.

Wally I'll remember you every day, as I'm sitting writing your postcards. (*Pause*) Shall we sit out here and watch the sun set?

May Don't be daft, we haven't had our lunches yet. Besides, the sun sets round the front.

Wally I know, May, but we can use our imaginations.

Wally puts his arm round May and she rests her head on his shoulder

The Lights fade to sunset red. Music: "Red Sails in the Sunset". The Lights fade to Black-out

Wally and May exit

The garden set is cleared and the lobby re-established

The Lights come up. It is night. There is moonlight at all the windows. George is in bed reading by the light of his bedside lamp

Wally enters along the corridor past Matron's office. He knocks at her door. There is silence. He goes to his room. He picks up his shell, then puts it down.

Wally Black-out zone, George. (*He leans over the line and switches off George's bedside lamp*)

George What's that for?

Wally Your own safety.

George switches the light back on

Fine, be an accomplice.

George switches it off. Wally shakes his shell. A small bunch of keys falls out. He picks them up

Your safety is assured.

George switches the light on

Wally goes to Matron's office, unlocks her door, enters and shuts the door. He opens the filing cabinet and riffles through

Wubblewoo for Wallis. Now ... pension book; ah. (*He finds and pockets it*) Passport. (*He finds it*) So many places. (*He holds it open on the desk and stamps it rapidly with his fist*) Oh, Mr Wally sahib. Welcome back. Very good. Very good. (*He pockets the passport and is about to leave but looks about, then turns the things on the desk around. He turns the chair that faces the desk, puts Matron's chair on top of the desk and as a parting gesture pops the palm plant into the filing cabinet and shuts the drawer with the palm sticking up*) There, Matron, I hope that takes your mind off some of your problems. (*He locks the door and creeps happily back to the room and straight over to George*) Listen George ... ah! (*He freezes; he has crossed the line*) I'm marooned in your sector. I've crossed the twilight zone — luckily I have an escape key. (*He puts a key on the tape, lifts up an end, walks through and resticks the tape. He walks down the correct side of the line, turns in at his bed, walks the path round his bed, puts the keys back in the shell and switches on his bedside lamp*) I came the scenic route. Ah home — just as I almost knew you. (*He walks high-wire style up the line, singing*) "He's daring and graceful in spite of his knees, That silly old coot on the flying trapeze. He does a back somersault ..." (*He prepares ... then sits on his bed*) George, I want to discuss a weakness of character. Mine not yours. I should have stayed earlier and sorted out this tape face to face — tried to see your point of view. I was weak and betrayed my principles and I want to apologize.

George You don't have to do that.

Wally I just did. Like wind — it's better out than in. I went to the doctor's once with wind — and he gave me a kite.

George I like kites.

Wally You would.

George I'm afraid this has been a somewhat inauspicious start for us. You probably think I've made rather a fool of myself.

Wally (*pulling a kitbag from under his bed*) A proper Charlie.

George I didn't expect sympathy.

Wally Look Colonel, this tape won't make your life easier, it'll give you nightmares I might put a toe over it.

George That's where you're wrong. The fact that I have a private world marked out will give me security. I'll feel safe. The division is for me — not you.

Wally I don't know anything about psychology. All I know is people do things to restrict themselves when they should be free.

George Most people are happier with the illusion of freedom than the reality.

Wally (*pulling a red ensign from the kitbag*) Ah, the old Red Duster. Potts and I use to raise this every evening. Our sun-down ceremony. Pure tradition. (*He sings "da" to "Rule Britannia" as he raises the flag in the window on strings fitted to the frame. He makes a ship's "Whoop Whoop" then a hooter sound and salutes the flag*) When it was all over we used to have a drink. Drink! If it's still there ...? (*He pulls back a curtain and finds a hiding place with a half-full bottle of whisky*) Hey hey. It's carnival time.

George You seem rather high-spirited tonight.
Wally I regained my sense of adventure. Colonel, get those glasses.

Wally ushers George out of bed

George The ones with our toothbrushes?
Wally Unless you brought the regimental crystal.
George (*collecting and wiping the glasses*) Why am I doing this?
Wally For one unrepeatable evening I am press-ganging you to WOR.
George War?
Wally W.O.R. Wally's Old Redoutables.
George What does it entail?
Wally Finishing the whisky.
George Oh, I don't know ...
Wally Now, George.
George Well you don't expect me to drink from this?
Wally Of course you're to drink from it, it's not a finger bowl. (*He pours whisky for them both*) George, we are drinking to the sea. To the borders it gives to our little island and to you — and the boundless promise it gives to me. The sea.
George The sea.

They toast and drink. George has not had a drink for some while

Wally Good on yer sport. That's brought the colour back to your cheeks.
George Thanks for the memory.
Wally Hey George, that Red Ensign, we used to fly that aft. That's the blunt end to you. I took it down on the last night of my last voyage and we sailed into Southampton flying a pair of the bosun's Y-fronts.

George laughs

Wasn't half a to-do. (*Singing a hornpipe*)
　　　　　　Oh, do your nuts hang low
　　　　　　Can you swing 'em to and fro ...
George Oh, I say ...
Wally (*going to the chest of drawers doing a sort of hornpipe; singing*)
　　　　　　Can you tie them in a reef knot
　　　　　　Can you tie them in a bow
　　　　　　Do you get a funny feeling
　　　　　　When you slap them on the ceiling
　　　　　　Oh, you'll never make a sailor if your nuts hang low.

They both laugh. George sits on Wally's bed. Wally takes out a drawer and takes it to his bed

Hey, George. Have you got your passport?
George (*rising*) Oh sorry. I'm over the limit. (*He returns to his side of the room*)
Wally (*whistling like a referee*) Yellow card. (*He goes to the wardrobe*) Come here a sec, Colonel, we've a bit of a problem.

George approaches the line

Stop. Mind how you cross the line, there might be a train coming.

George crosses

You see, George, your door has to be opened before I can get to my clothes.

George opens "his" door

Well we should do this properly. I'd hate to get a royal invitation when you're out and I need my dicky suit in a hurry. (*He takes out his suit on a hanger*) Look at that; an original from War on Want.

George sits. As Wally talks he folds his suit and stuffs it into the kitbag

I had this suit made up in Hong Kong. "Sam's Tailors". Only took a day. Eight quid, that's all. Beautiful material. Real craftsmanship. Forty years I've had it. But do you know, I've only worn it once. It doesn't fit.

They laugh. Wally finishes packing the suit and packs clothes from the drawer

I had a dinner jacket made the same time. Beautiful dinner jacket — black facings. Two fittings in a day. I went to a dance in Hong Kong that night and the Skipper walked in. I went: "Sir". (*He salutes*) And the sleeve fell off.

They laugh. Wally continues packing

George Why are you putting your clothes in there?
Wally Matron takes in laundry.
George (*going to a drawer*) How splendid.
Wally You've got some fancy ideas. I'm leaving, George. Not being rude but you and I couldn't share this matchbox in a month of Sundays.

George Oh please, that makes me feel awful. Which room are you going to? I'll speak to Mrs Winstanley and move there instead.

Wally I'm leaving the home, George. The room hasn't changed, you dividing it up has shown me the restrictions that have been placed on me. There were no boundaries with Potts: he was like the sea, everlasting. As he can't travel much now, I thought I'd take his spirit with me. Do you think spirits get seasick?

George You're not considering going back to sea?

Wally Why not? I'm too old for ships but summer's coming on. I'll find a nice little southern berth to somewhere. I can mend engines, repair sails, burnish brass brighter than the sun, and do a leetle French cooking on a stove no bigger than that. We old sea dogs are popular for our antique curiosity. Like dusty log books full of fascinating stories.

George But you retired years ago.

Wally Well I'm retiring from retirement. I've had enough of sleeping in a bed that doesn't move. (*He gets the whisky bottle*)

George You make me feel guilty, Mr Wallis.

Wally Wally, Colonel. We're drinking together.

George Wally — as if I'm driving you away.

Wally pours a measure into George's glass

That's not very much.

Wally (*adding more*) You've soon got the hang of this.

George Thank you. I mean, how will you manage? It's stating the obvious but you're no longer young.

Wally refills his own glass and sits on his bed facing George

Wally Colonel, you mustn't look on this old age thing as an end: it isn't an end, it's a beginning. As much a beginning as any other time in your life. People are always telling you how quickly it goes; how short life it is. Well, short compared to what? A tree? A turtle? Seventy — eighty years, that doesn't seem too short to me. But it is short if you start looking back with regret. Remembering the days when you should have ... the days when you almost ... . You'll be all right here, Colonel. You'll fit in, I never did.

George You may be right. The life I cared about was over long ago. Since I retired, and still more since my wife died, I've been an observer rather than a participant. So all I need is a comfortable observation post with all mod-cons and this place should fit the bill. It begins to feel like home.

Wally They call it home but it's still an institution. A breaker's yard for rusting old hulks.

George Well my joints certainly need oiling but otherwise I feel much as I did thirty years ago.

Wally What's the point of an agile mind if the body can't keep up. I want the lot to go at once. And somewhere at sea will suit me well. With Potts' spirit and my body who knows where we'll end up.

George What will you do for money?

Wally Ah. My Fairy Godmother visited me during a moment of euphoria — and showered me with gold. (*He pulls the chain from his pocket*)

George (*proposing a toast*) Well here's to your Fairy Godmother.

Wally Indeed. My Fairy Godmother. (*He toasts and drinks*) God bless her.

George God bless her. (*He finishes his whisky*) I feel quite merry.

Wally Not before time.

George My wife would have enjoyed herself tonight.

Wally (*uncertainly*) Yes.

George is now tiddly. He rises and, copying Wally's "Hornpipe", dances over to the chest of drawers to put his glass

George (*singing*) Do your nuts hang low
                Can you swing them to and fro ...
  (*Speaking*) How does it go after that?

Wally Hey, George .... Da da la da da ...

Wally starts a proper Hornpipe. George copies. They "Da Da La ..." and dance two choruses, ending up going faster and round each other with arms linked in a hearty climax. Then they hold on to each other laughing. Wally moves giddily away and sits on his bed

I'll be glad when we dock.

George sways

(*Getting up and stopping George from falling*) Easy, George. Easy. Come on.

George Is it bedtime yet?

Wally Yes, Colonel, I think it is.

Wally guides George over to his bed and he lies on top of it still in dressing-gown, pyjamas and slippers. His feet hang off the end

We might have to take a bit off your legs. (*He turns off George's lamp, goes to his own bed and takes off his shoes*)

George (*singing drunkenly*) "Do your nuts hang low, can you swinggle le da de ..." (*He laughs*)

Wally I've got an early start tomorrow, so I'll be up before the birds. (*He wonders about undressing*) Matthew, Mark, Luke and John — went to bed with their trousers on.

George (*giggling*) But they took their shirts off — didn't they?
Wally Not tonight.

Wally nips into bed and turns off his light. Moonlight floods Wally's side of the line

   Good-night Colonel.
George Good-night Wally.
Wally (*after a pause*) Colonel?
George Yes.
Wally I hope you don't mind but the moonlight is on my side of the line.

Pause

George Wally.
Wally Yes, Colonel.
George I became an expert on camouflage in the jungle.
Wally (*sitting up and looking*) Well. That'll be very handy in here. When you want some peace and quiet. (*He lies down*)
George If you escape from Grove Lodge now I could put some boot polish on your face.
Wally (*sitting up*) What the hell would you want to do that for?
George So you'd blend in with the night.
Wally I don't think I'd get away with impersonating Al Jolson. My bus pass photo doesn't do him justice. (*He lies down*)

Pause

George Wally? (*Beat*) Wally? (*Louder*) Wally!
Wally Yes, Colonel.
George Are you asleep?
Wally No. I just fainted for a minute.
George I thought you'd want to know, I'm sorry you're going. I've enjoyed tonight.
Wally Don't mention it. So have I.

There is a slight pause

George Marjorie ...
Wally (*sitting up*) Hey hey, none of that.
George No: did I make the right choice? Between her and the regiment.
Wally Yes, Colonel. Yes, I think you did. Oh, and Colonel: over and out. (*He pulls the covers around him*)

The Lights fade to Black-out. Music. The Lights come up

Tuesday. A sunny morning

The music fades. An ambulance siren is heard departing

   Matron enters her office, looks at the chaos then checks the door lock

At the same time, Wally pops his legs out of bed. He can reach the basin from here and he turns on the tap, gets his hand wet, wipes it across his face and dries it. Matron goes to the room and knocks on the door

Wally Come in if you're beautiful. (*He finishes drying and hangs up the towel*)

Matron enters and goes up to him at the basin

   You weren't listening, cheeky.
Matron (*coolly*) Good-morning Mr Wallis.
Wally Indeed it is, my Matron, indeed it is.
Matron Unlike you to be up early.
Wally I'm set fair with a following wind.
Matron May I have a word with you in my office?
Wally Today, Matron, you can have as many words as you fancy.
Matron This room is a disgrace. And what's happened to him?
Wally Ah, George. Half a cup of Ovaltine and he goes wild.
Matron Falling into bad habits early on.
Wally Just falling asleep I think.
Matron (*sniffing George's glass*) This smells of alcohol.
Wally That's my mouthwash. Very pure.
Matron (*seeing the tape*) And what is all this?
Wally Someone's idea of home improvements.
Matron I agreed to moving a little furniture. I suppose this tape is your idea.
Wally Mine ... !
Matron If this carpet has bald stripes you'll pay for it. You'd better come to my office as you are.
Wally I'll just give George a gentle shake first.

Matron leaves to the lobby

   (*Clanging the ship's bell and adopting a Sergeant's voice*) Heeeyuuup. Show a leg, you scruffy Midshipman. Didn't you hear eight bells, you unshaven reprobate?
George (*holding his head*) Is there a fire?
Wally (*sweetly patting George's head*) Not yet. I'm just going up to see the Gauleiter. (*He leaves the room*)

Matron meets Wally in the lobby

Matron Haven't you any slippers? You'll get chilblains.
Wally My feet are too cold to get them.
Matron (*opening her door*) After you.

Wally enters Matron's office and ignores the changes. She expects some comment but he just looks pleasantly at her. They look at the chair on her desk

Wally D'you want a leg up?

Matron takes the chair off the desk and sits

During the following George finds a moment to rise unobtrusively, with quite a "head". He puts a towel round his shoulders and lathers to shave

Matron I received a phone call this morning from the undertaker. You were quite right in your opinion of Mr Potterton's niece, she has totally abrogated herself of any responsibility. A callous woman. Well, naturally the undertaker asked for my instructions and as you were closest to Mr Potterton, I wondered which you would prefer?
Wally Prefer?
Matron Burial or cremation.
Wally Oh. Potts looked so peaceful lying there it seems a shame we can't just leave him.
Matron Yes, well Mr Trueit cannot manage a burial until Friday. But he could arrange a cremation at noon today.
Wally That's a bit quick.
Matron He's had a cancellation.
Wally Did one of his customers recover?
Matron The family converted to the soil but there won't be a hole until Wednesday.
Wally A hole. Oh. We always talked about burial at sea. That was his last wish.
Matron The Council won't run to that.
Wally It's standard procedure in the navy.
Matron You're not in the navy, you're in here.
Wally It needn't be elaborate.
Matron It's out of the question.
Wally What kind of seaside town is it that doesn't offer burial at sea?
Matron We live on an island. Why discriminate against the Midlands?
Wally All right then, a river. As long as it's tidal.
Matron No.

Wally A man should be buried where he wants.
Matron No doubt he can be if you're paying.
Wally (*considering the gold chain in his pocket*) Are ashes heavy?
Matron Not particularly.
Wally Better be cremated then.
Matron I'll inform Mr Trueit.
Wally I've never been to a cremation.
Matron My husband was cremated.
Wally Did you do it?

Matron looks stonily at Wally

(*Back-pedalling and sitting*) I never thought of you as being married.
Matron Twenty-one long years. He was much older than I. (*Pause*) At the cremation the vicar said to me, "Do not agonize over his departure — you will meet again in heaven." I thought, I hope to God I don't because I've had enough of him here.
Wally (*smiling*) Funny, isn't it ... ?
Matron What is?
Wally The things people don't know about each other. You ... (*He makes a lovey-dovey gesture*) Will they send a car for me?
Matron You can get straight there on the bus.
Wally I'll persuade the driver to follow the hearse.
Matron You're taking this very well, Mr Wallis.
Wally Fresh lease of life. Potts would have been the same if it had been me.
Matron Yes I expect he would. Well, I'll let you know the arrangements after breakfast.
Wally Thank you. (*He moves to leave, stopping at the door*) Oh and Matron, I like the way you've done your office. (*He nips out, shuts the door and heads for the room*)

Matron looks out after Wally, then exits

Wally enters the room. George still has the towel over his shoulders and his face is heavily lathered

Morning Santa. How's the head?
George Awful.
Wally The true sign of a good night.
George I can't see what I've lathered.
Wally Then don't use the razor. A mistake could be lethal. (*He picks up Potts' mug*) Colonel, I don't want this to break. Could you wrap it for me?

George wraps the mug in a towel. Wally sits beside him and puts on his shoes

George You're still going then?

Wally More important than yesterday. They're cremating Potts today. As the Council are too mean to bury him at sea I shall take his ashes and bury him there myself. We liked unusual ways of starting adventures. Potts had a favourite island in the Pacific. I can't remember the actual name but it translates as Land of Gentle Breezes. That's where I'll take him. Scatter his ashes in the sea that washes his island.

George You should find a box for this mug if you're going to be moving about.

Wally (*packing the mug in the kitbag*) Yes I will. I suppose I might want to read.(*He drops the paperbacks in his kitbag and picks* Jane's Fighting Ships *off the shelf. It is so heavy he almost topples. He weighs it up*) I want you to have this.

George (*thrilled*) It's brand new.

Wally No, I've looked at the pictures. It was our moving in present, so it sort of belongs to the room.

George Thank you. I'll look after it for you.

Wally Yes I know you will. (*He looks about*) I want to travel light so everything I haven't packed, you can have. The trunk. This shell, you can have that. You put that shell to your ear and you can hear the sea. But you have to be standing on the beach. Oh and Colonel, keep this flag flying as long as you are in residence.

George Yes, of course.

Wally (*tightening the kitbag*) That's it. I'm all ready for cast off.

George (*taking the flowers from the vase*) Why don't you take these for Mr Potterton.

Wally Won't they recognize them at the crematorium?

George There's no label.

Wally He liked flowers. (*He places the flowers on the kitbag then spits on his hands and slicks his hair*)

George No no no.

Wally I'm just making myself look presentable.

George (*offering his comb*) You'll look more presentable if you use this. Please: a swap for the book.

Wally Oh ... (*He takes the comb and combs his hair, eyebrows and under his arms*)

They both laugh

The breakfast bell rings loudly

George I'm not even dressed.

Wally You're not even shaved. Never mind, George, I'll look after you. (*He wipes the foam from George's face with the towel*) You don't want to miss today's breakfast. It's BTM day.

George BTM?

Wally Beans This Morning. And remember you're entitled to thirty-eight. (*He makes a corner in the towel and cleans George's ear like a child*) There.

May enters the room

May Have you heard about Mr Gomez?

George Not another flood?

May No. Another heart attack.

Wally What, two in a week? That's messed up my sweepstake.

George What a heartless thing to say.

Wally Unfortunately heartless is just what it wasn't.

May Poor Mr Gomez.

They have a moment's silence

(*To George*) Did you know he had the single room next to mine?

They all look from one to the other, knowing what this implies

Wally You wanton woman.

May Wanton nothing. What's the good of living if you haven't got something to look forward to. You're off — and I haven't time to waste.

Wally Ay, ay, Colonel. I think your ship's come in.

George It would allow them to decorate this place. (*He looks at his/Potts' bed*)

May What's the matter, George?

George I was just thinking, if I took Mr Gomez' room it wouldn't do much for my reputation.

May Well, thank you.

George No, no, I only meant — for stepping into dead men's shoes.

Wally Cor blimey!

George I had the same reputation in the army.

Wally (*to May*) I better send your postcards first class. (*He goes to May*) Goodbye, Fairy Godmother.

May Goodbye, dear Wally.

Wally kisses May's forehead

Matron enters

Matron Loitering again, May. Now I'm definitely ordering you that Zimmer frame.

May Scaffolding be buggered. I'll have a bath chair sometimes as a treat. And an army officer to push me round.

George twirls the towel on to his bed and strides forward

Matron Not dressed like that, Major. Black mark.

Matron exits

May and George smile at each other

May sings a line from "Isn't It a Lovely Day to Be Caught in the Rain", clicks her tongue twice and exits to the dining area with George following

Wally puts on his coat and hat, picks up his kitbag and the flowers and looks around, saying his goodbye to the room. He moves to the door, lifts the flowers to salute the room and heads for the fire exit

George enters

George Aren't you coming in to breakfast, Wally?
Wally No I've got to catch the tide.
George You sure you'll be all right?
Wally Yes, we'll be fine.
George We?
Wally Me and Potts. Well, his ashes. Oh George, do me a favour. Will you keep Captain Bligh off my scent till after the cremation.
George Fill in at roll call you mean. Certainly.
Wally You'd better not hang about. If you're late in the dining-room Wiggins will have you shot as a deserter.
George I'm not afraid of Wiggins. She was only a Corporal in the ATS. Good luck, Wally. (*He offers his hand*)
Wally (*shaking George's hand*) Goodbye, Colonel. (*He shoulders his kitbag*) Look after my May.
George Of course.
Wally Oh, and run a tight ship here.
George Ay, ay, sir.
Wally You'll do.

Wally opens the fire exit door and exits

George watches him go and waves. May's voice offstage interrupts him

May (*saucily; off*) Major.

George snaps to attention

Music begins: "Grenadier Guards"

> *George turns and marches off towards the dining-room*

CURTAIN

Curtain call music: "A Life on the Ocean Wave" or similar

PRODUCTION NOTE

THE CHAPEL OF REST SCENE (P. 30)

This play may be performed without the Chapel of Rest setting. The alternative scene takes place in the garden and is played reflectively as if Wally has just returned from visiting Potts in the Chapel of Rest. It also allows the garden to be set, unlit, from the beginning of the act, if preferred

ALTERNATIVE SCENE

The Lights come up on the garden. Birdsong, including the sound of gulls, can be heard; this fades as the scene begins

Wally enters, sits on the bench and pulls off his hat. The Lights fade except on Wally, isolating him

Wally Oh Pottsy. If only I could have said what I felt just now. You looked so good, old friend. Better than you did in life. Not that your old body knows much now. Your pain has gone. Mine's just beginning. I know — don't be morbid. Death is only God's way of telling you to "sod off". Remember how we used to sit out here in the mornings? Everyone saying nice things to you. Hasn't changed. Matron clearly wishes I was in your place. Nurse Wiggins shook my hand and nearly dislocated my thumb. She's going to carry the coffin — by herself. Oh, Potts, we had the whole world living in our minds, now it's deserted. Is it too late to talk about love? I know you loved everyone, that was your gift to life, but you even made me feel loved, nobody's done that before: I didn't know how to respond. My love's always been for nature's things: the sea, open sky, the cry of the seagulls. I never knew about love for people. Your way. If it's not too late — I'd like to say I love you. I don't know how, Potts, but somehow I'll find a way of taking you with me. Perhaps that will give me the strength to carry on. (*He touches the bench where Potts would have sat*) Goodbye, old friend. My only other life.

The birdsong fades up

Wally exits

The Lights fade to Black-out

FURNITURE AND PROPERTY LIST

ACT I

On stage: WALLY'S ROOM
Two easy chairs
Two divan beds. *On shelf by* **Wally***'s bed*: three worn paperbacks, *Jane's Fighting Ships*, large seashell containing key, photo. *Under* **Wally***'s bed*: old trunk containing packet of cigarettes, shrunken head, small electric stove (practical), spatula, meat fork. Kitbag containing red ensign. Chamber pot containing herbs and condiments. *On shelf by other bed*: garish beer mug, soccer scarf
Double wardrobe. *On it*: plate. *In it*: hangers, **Wally**'s clothes including suit. *Behind panels*: bottle of whisky, bottle of oil, two slices of bread
Chest of drawers. *In it*: frying pan, various items of underwear
Waste-basket
By sink: towel
Bedside lamps (practical)

LOBBY
Hall table
Large, smart suitcase containing two family photographs, framed display of medals, detective novels, blazer, trousers, shirts, ties, journal, shoe trees, shoes

OFFICE
Palm
Filing cabinet. *On it*: attaché case. *In it*: **Wally**'s pension book and passport
Desk. *In drawer*: pill
Chairs
Jug of water and glass
Hat and furled umbrella for **George**

Off stage: Clipboard (**Matron**)
Vase of flowers (**Matron**)
Steak wrapped in paper (**Wally**)
Piece of cake on plate (**May**)
Two cups of tea (**George**)
Plate of toast (**May**)

Personal: **Matron**: pager (worn throughout)
May: stick (used throughout), gold locket (worn throughout)
Wally: pot of Vick, red spotted handkerchief

ACT II

Strike: WALLY'S ROOM
             All **Wally**'s cooking equipment

             LOBBY
             Hall table

Set: WALLY'S ROOM
             Initials on furniture
             White tape dividing room (see p. 29)
             Roll of tape for **George**
             Note
             Cassette/radio
             Half-full bottle of whisky behind curtain
             George's shaving materials

             LOBBY
             Chapel of Rest setting
             Coffin

Off stage: Cup of coffee, saucer (**George**)
             Pillow (**Matron**)

During scene starting p. 31

Strike: Chapel of Rest setting

Set: Garden setting — flower-covered trellis or wall
             Rustic bench

During scene starting p. 39

Strike: Garden setting and bench

Set: Hall table

LIGHTING PLOT

Practical fittings required: bedside lamps
Three interiors — bedroom, lobby, office — with exterior backing behind windows.
Chapel of Rest and Garden sets in place of lobby in Act II

ACT I

To open: General interior lighting on all areas; morning effect

Cue 1	**George** puts the steak on the plate *Fade lights in room*	(Page 8)
Cue 2	**Wally** leaves the office and shuts the door *Bring up lights in room*	(Page 10)
Cue 3	**Wally** cuddles the glass, sobbing gently *Fade all lights*	(Page 12)
Cue 4	When ready *Bring up all lights; afternoon effect*	(Page 12)
Cue 5	**George** sits down to read a journal *Fade lights on room*	(Page 15)
Cue 6	**Matron** exits towards the dining area *Bring up lights on room*	(Page 16)
Cue 7	**George** watches **Wally** uncertainly *Fade all lights*	(Page 16)
Cue 8	Sound of electronic church bells *Bring up all lights; morning effect*	(Page 18)
Cue 9	**May** exits; **George** remains, bemused *Cross-fade lights to evening setting*	(Page 21)

ACT II

To open: Lights up on room with sunny effect on exterior backing; no lights on Chapel of Rest or Office

Cue 10	**May**: "... he comes back and sees it." *Fade all lights to black-out*	(Page 30)
Cue 11	Quiet organ music *Bring up Chapel of Rest lighting with sepulchral glow on* **Wally**	(Page 30)
Cue 12	**Wally** exits *Fade all lights to black-out*	(Page 31)

Alternative Scene

Cue 11a	When ready *Bring up lights on garden*	(Page 53)
Cue 12a	**Wally** pulls off his hat *Fade lights except on* **Wally**	(Page 53)
Cue 13a	**Wally** exits *Fade to black-out; then Cue* 13	(Page 53)

Cue 13	When ready *Bring up lights on room and corridor*	(Page 31)
Cue 14	**George** throws the hat on **Wally**'s bed *Fade lights on room*	(Page 33)
Cue 15	Music *Bring up lights on garden setting*	(Page 33)
Cue 16	**Mary** rests her head on **Wally**'s shoulder *Fade lights to sunset red*	(Page 39)
Cue 17	Music: *"Red Sails in the Sunset"* *Fade lights to black-out*	(Page 39)
Cue 18	When ready *Bring up night-time lighting effect, with moonlight and practical bedside lamps*	(Page 39)

Cue 19   **Wally** pulls the covers around him   (Page 46)
             Fade all lights to black-out

Cue 20   When ready   (Page 46)
             Bring up all lights; sunny morning effect

EFFECTS PLOT

ACT I

Cue 1	**Matron**: "That's what counts." *Pager bleeps*	(Page 3)
Cue 2	**Wally** cuddles the glass; the lights fade *Music*	(Page 12)
Cue 3	The lights come up *Music fades; electronic tea bell rings*	(Page 12)
Cue 4	The lights fade, then come up again *Peals of church bells segue into electronic church bells*	(Page 17)
Cue 5	**Wally**: "That explains a lot." *Electronic church bells*	(Page 18)
Cue 6	**Wally** opens the door *Congregation and harmonium as p.18*	(Page 18)
Cue 7	**Matron** (*off*): " — 'What a Friend We Have in Jesus.'" *Congregation and harmonium*	(Page 19)
Cue 8	**May** looks at **George** cheekily *Music*	(Page 21)
Cue 9	**George** starts to wash his hands *Music fades*	(Page 21)
Cue 10	**Wally** exits *Music*	(Page 28)

ACT II

Cue 11	The lights change to Chapel of Rest setting *Quiet organ music*	(Page 30)
Cue 12	**Wally** pulls off his hat *Music fades*	(Page 30)

| *Cue* 13 | **Wally**: "My only other life."
*Music fades up; segue into military march
from George's radio* | (Page 30) |

Alternative Scene

| *Cue* 11a | The lights come up on the garden
Birdsong, including gulls; fade when established | (Page 53) |

| *Cue* 12a | **Wally**: "My only other life."
*Birdsong fades up; segue into military march
as per Cue 13* | (Page 53) |

| *Cue* 14 | **George** shuts the bedroom door
Military music gets quieter | (Page 31) |

| *Cue* 15 | **Wally** opens the door
Music gets louder | (Page 31) |

| *Cue* 16 | **Wally** flicks the music off
Cut music | (Page 31) |

| *Cue* 17 | The lights fade on **George**
Music | (Page 33) |

| *Cue* 18 | The lights come up on **May**
Music fades | (Page 33) |

| *Cue* 19 | The lights fade to sunset red
Music: "Red Sails in the Sunset"; fade when ready | (Page 39) |

| Cue 20 | The lights fade to black-out
Music | (Page 46) |

| *Cue* 21 | The lights come up
Music fades: ambulance siren — departing | (Page 46) |

| *Cue* 22 | **George** and **Wally** laugh
Breakfast bell rings loudly | (Page 49) |

| *Cue* 23 | **George** snaps to attention
Music: "Grenadier Guards" | (Page 52) |

| *Cue* 24 | Curtain calls
Music: "A Life on the Ocean Wave" | (Page 52) |